2009

k
&

All ou.
Ma & Pa
x x x
o o o

security posture

security posture

Sarah Dowling

SNARE BOOKS . MONTREAL

Edited by Rachel Zolf
Cover designed by Jon Paul Fiorentino
Guts designed by Leigh Kotsilidis
Copyedited by Marisa Grizenko
Typeset in Garamond and Rockwell

Library and Archives Canada Cataloguing in Publication

Dowling, Sarah, 1982-
    Security posture : poetry / Sarah Dowling.

ISBN 978-0-9812488-2-0

    I. Title.

PS8607.O9875S43 2009   C811'.6   C2009-904454-4

Printed and bound in Canada
Represented in Canada by the Literary Press Group
Distributed by LitDistCo

SNARE BOOKS
4832A Parc Avenue
Montreal QC
H2V 4E6
snarebooks.wordpress.com

Canada Council   Conseil des Arts
for the Arts   du Canada

Snare Books gratefully acknowledges the financial support of the Canada Council for the Arts.

Note paper, white linen. A row of buttons and the roaring of waves. Wouldn't it just stop. Birds' shadows across the pavement, fast, silent. Closer. She says her hand in her hair. Suddenly, the square is dark.

purports to wick it

and so tenderly

until everything

stop up the ears

If she lay down on the ground

       went ahead to

       structure it all disappeared

the she of hold, she of thrall
the thrall in which others

       rolled over and

       lost   something done

If she lay on her back and thralled

       what she lost she st

       to cause

lost sight of her
   all of   and

       if she was rolled over

       with others, with fearing

If she lay down

        disappeared from the sh

        like a shadow, like

thrall from the ground her
shoulders and

        go on and was rolled

        about what she

If she lay and fearing

        and lost sight of

        and back

and down like a shadow, all of her

        rolled her structure

        thrall, and   disappear

Cotton hand. Wouldn't it just loose. Then camisole, white shorts.
Streetlight through the concrete. Shoulders, hair. Even curtains
stop.

            and is there a way

            stuffed this

            kind of punctuated

            of what is heard

If she was made to

cut back

with all of it

cut back to assurance
, made to do

a hand

and just go on

If she lost sight of this

of the ground

all of it moving

the back so cut
the structure until

this hand

which

If she laid there

        what cut

        what lost

stuck with assurance
with surety and all of it

        back like this to go

          the ground, all over

what would have made her

        would have made

        this

    surety of thrall
in response in which

         response cut

        back response

Series of water. Even, then softly movement. The hand just wouldn't waves, wouldn't hair. Fast, not so much falling as clothing. Not so much flying as silent.

and if they can't

that have been threatened

is rendered

wax

If she lost sight of it

        lay her back and ahead

        around

on her back she lost the thrall in which
if her, if structure

        if all of her

        in which, if hold

If   on the ground others

        went ahead to st

        to thrall

made it until she   and hold her
back all of her sh

        until how hold

        in it, in

Woven, thickly pressed. The skin becoming wouldn't. Shadow on the pavement, shoulder and loose. A darkened square. Stop, like the roaring of waves.

pulled off hard

or slowly

stopped up

in the very same

This I will never be able to narrate.

As the back seat is remembered because of a detail.

As if without doubt, without knowledge
a gesture will tell it.

As if from memory, a subject, from pulsing. As if
from childhood. From ecstasy, from a fall
from words. As if from the body differently.

As if between tenderness a series of gestures
that constitute the body in writing/writhing

and compel

This was not a caress.

With eyes on the water makes
you suddenly turn around her
arm, her legs splash up. Fastidious,
the sea not yet blank and sullen
taken into suddenly. Her
back a bare body
calling on the water.

The fulfillment

This was   .

        Here
        was the almost. Arm her
        eyes on the water, legs
        about to call
        to take touch. With a bare
        little surge your body up your back
        turn around if not suddenly.

as assurance.

This   .

    The sea almost
    within. Splash calling up
    at you here on your arm, on
    your legs your eyes
    about the water. As if suddenly
    body, blank and
    sullen. Taken
    not yet bare with anyone.

The way you

not a care .

Yet it had nothing, eyes
in the sea. Calling an
arm and legs about to surge
up. Not yet. Turn around
taken in fastidious
eyes and then bare
herself on the water.

control

"security posture"   evidence
                            found in the way you

                            control

                            your response spread out
                            evening when I turn it

                            palatable
                            assurance

                            fulfillment of obligation
                            of another, a surety

not a caress.

Calling to here, her sullen
blank legs taking this
within eyes in
water. About to surge your
back almost. Touch
made you suddenly
turn her this armed you
here.

another, a sure .

Meanwhile as the back seat, women. This dark
blue persists as the body dictates its clichés
writhing closes its eyes its mouths that open
to repetition, touched
within their movement. A series of gestures

as always evasive. A thought begins
in the mouth, plays as memory back
against seat into hand as face over
turning through.

Scene as a series of actions. In relief,
strokes of the body,

Once a wind comes up and goes away suddenly.

> could wrap a treetop
> grasp
>
> wrapped around as if clinging
> to as if bent against
> broken in some
>
> > thing strewn or
> > blown before
>
> warning
>
> osage oranges
> falling
>
> each having
> its own

Once I heard it.

Once, it   .

       some one
       that continues to

       does it work that
         , falling

       before or there

       putting hands over

                                     the side

        s   because an answer

       evenly

       distributed underf

Once it brings certain   and takes away

Once it   th   s.

    made a

        and
    inaccessible because

                                            yourself

    where I was sleeping
    wrapped some

    and only happening once,

wants
such a
that it's always

somewhere

or there,

just

stop

Once the car st   the lights   .

the s

touching
on wants

this

will want
to   some other

even your

, work
that   because
each having
its own

,   are touching.

                                        stand

        as if clinging
        to an evenness
         covered, like

absent

whatever type of
falling, other times

yourself

a treetop or leaves

like

or blown

Once the door is   and   st .

Once I am c

    Before

       this
       tangles, st

            where something

    pries

       itself
          is pried

    and the radio clicks   ,

Meanwhile as what makes her say: It's late.

Makes rough and senseless. Makes extravagance
of surfaces this transparency that the body carries
within itself relive in a set of decisive gestures.
Makes a movement of hand toward

clothing that intervenes
and conforms exactly.
Makes the tension of skins' extreme concentration.

Makes hand toward grasping against

the narrow movement
    w i   /   thin a memory

sky, the against
is spread out evening when
I turn over
there I turn
myself, like
stones

soft white walls
you are my *assurance*
f
you, everyday
turn, pass her delicate *may I*

pool I leave it
turn you're what
like stones f
the against like
f

f
like against the
f stones like
what you're turn
it leave I pool

I may delicate her pass, turn
everyday, you
f
my *response* are you
walls white soft

stones
like, myself
turn I there
over turn I
when evening out spread is
against the, sky

f like f what it
I everyday, f my *control* walls
stones like, turn over when against

against stones you're leave
may you are white
myself I turn evening, the

the like turn I
delicate you you soft
there I out sky

pool
her
spread

pass,
is
turn

"securit   "   obligation
                                      found in evidence of

                                          in assurance

                                  in the
                                  you

                                  are your
                                              , given

                        ·   another, given
                            surety

turn
is
pass,

spread
her
pool

sky out there I
soft you you delicate
I turn like the

the evening, turn I myself
white are *you may*
leave you're stones against

against when over turn like, stones
walls my *palatable* f everyday, I
it what f like f

turn spread sky soft I the white leave against walls *it*
is her out you turn evening are you're when my *surety* what
pass pool I you like turn you stones over f f
there delicate the I may against turn everyday like
myself like, everyday, f
stones

falling

the knot of it
a kind of sleeping
under-
f   ,

                                        the side of

Once a wind comes up and goes away suddenly

stones
f everyday, like, myself
like everyday *turn against* may I the delicate there
f f over stones you turn like you I pool pass
what my *fulfillment* when you   evening turn you out her is
it walls against leave white the I soft sky spread turn

Meanwhile that stretches bodies outward.

/writhing eyes
darken. The pleasure of audacity
as a gesture that clothes a memory
containing only transparency, skins
more. These

pulsing forward
continue   .

A detail so specific as meaningless, remembered
differently a series of actions as intense
and senseless, this

I will never be able to narrate

"s u   re"   fulfillment as

                              , the way you
                    turn

                    like   ,
          I turn

          your response
            control

          turn evening
          palatable

: hairs :

and all these restrictions are single
but for some
reason or another
whether clenched a white

: tile :

it cannot float but
gently she when submerged they
flagellate individually
here at my

: trivial :

when the hairs
makes no difference

: furtive :

only because they are wet

: hairs :

the place on which the mouth
clenched she
her clenched muscles that
encloses the back
and sides

: with which :

when should I turn over in
the water the dress, I

: but now :

one fragment the fabric the
hairs are separately she
privacy and myself

: unfurl :

: hairs :

no difference
whether your eyes are
opens the furtive and girlish

: are wet :

so gradually a soft

: tension :

the water the hairs warp
apart but cling together when
removed from

: bruiseless :

and one long strand but
for some other
dress as if I should

: hairs :

removed from together
the hairs
clings when its
she your eyes
are open a person across

: whose :

seemed as if I
dress apart of
should

: who is :

with bits of
those who have played with
wet the marks I
clinging on the tiles

: the floor :

: hairs :

and close a red
your eyes in
moves a white
tile floor

: whose dress :

had seemed a part

: they cling :

pinkish unfurl and all these
removed from the

: the limbs of :

hair that spread on the
the one apart a

"   "   evidence of security
                            found

                                in the

                                    soft
                            I turn

                                    myself
                            in the

It is not given to each of us

                                                        throught

hold hurt all flesh
as sill "as much"
than gale the leaves
the deepest traces

                                              not moving "hair"
                                              as crisp to mouth

an alley

the finding

                                                        desired

56

lamp

"than sill" sleeveless
how much they find
as hard, rather cold
with posture

hair held
"as mouth"
"to shoulder"

trail

refinding

"what flesh," how much

                                              they
                                              field

"what recourse"

      lamp and

                                        "shoulders"

                                          crisp

            gale   given

                                        what recourse

hurt
throught

                                                    than
                                                        hurt than

                                                    traces

shoulders

to each, how leaves
not moving

                                                in   cold

                                        in fact

"it is not"

                                    rather, the alley
                                the   lamp

    sleeve and shoulder
        left the deepest

            finding "as hard"
                                            field

        finding

                                            left

                        all flesh,

                                    f

the finding of it

held posture

as recourse
traces

gale as a passing

leaves
than   "   cold"
with   held

hurt
moving
"left" traces

given, not

rather, "f   "

The word written on the white wall

    noirceur, visible only in headlights.

This as the detail that makes bodies taut
makes all of the blood ache

and surge forward.

This as the detail of dark blue interior
of seats, tension, pluming snow
        , of hands unspeakably
stopped car.

        Meanwhile
    /writh   .

Acknowledgements

This book is for my family, my friends, and all of my teachers, with much love.

Many thanks to everyone who has supported my work at readings, especially Jena Osman, Rachel Blau DuPlessis, Frank Sherlock, CAConrad, Emily Abendroth, Justin Audia, Ryan Eckes, a.rawlings, Jessica Lowenthal and Al Filreis, and everyone at the Kelly Writers House. I also thank Jenn McCreary and Chris McCreary, and François Luong for publishing earlier versions of this work in *the ixnay reader 4*, and *Action Yes!*, respectively. Deepest gratitude to Divya Victor and Jason Zuzga for being compassion-ate friends and readers, to Julia Bloch and Janet Neigh for being committed thinkers and fellow travelers, and to Pattie McCarthy, Kevin Varrone, and Emmett and Asher for all their kindness. Thanks to Charles Bernstein, Heather Love, Josephine Park, and Bob Perelman for unknowingly planting the seeds of this project. And most especially, thanks to Rachel Zolf, whose generous and attentive editing helped me shape *Security Posture* into what I wanted it to be.

Everything to my parents, everything to my sisters, everything to my friends, as ever.